Title: Dear Syd...
Author: Jubilee Mosley
Illustrator: WWR Graphics

Dedication

To Sydney Judah Mosley, the youngest, funniest, and most charismatic teacher I've ever met.

Thanks for teaching me to turn my reality into my dreams.

Dear Syd,

please don't take your sock off
and use it to wipe your mouth after
eating.

5

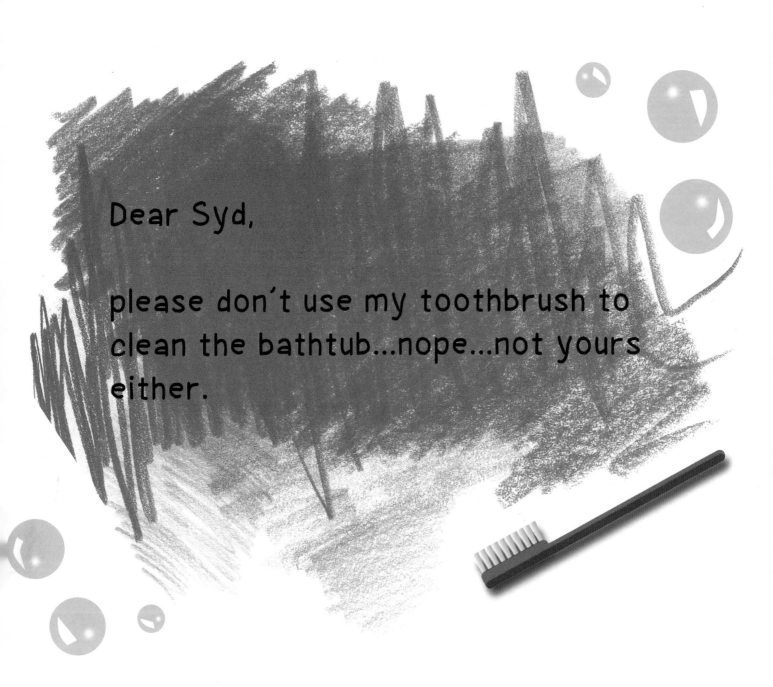

Dear Syd,

please don't use my toothbrush to clean the bathtub...nope...not yours either.

Dear Syd,

Please don't use the vacuum brush
to brush your hair.

Dear Syd,

Thanks for singing to Zach in your infamous falsetto voice. The ABC's and Twankle, Twankle little Starr will never be the same...and neither will Zach.

Dear Syd,

Please...don't call your father "Babe".

13

Dear Syd,

I love when you say "Go Mommy, go, go, go" when I'm dancing. You make me feel so cool!

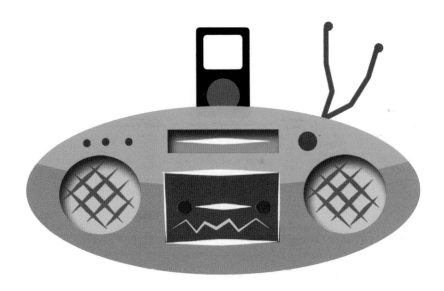

Dear Syd,

Thank you for randomly singing into your nasal aspirator and playing your mini "titar", You really are a great performer!

17

Dear Syd,

Thank you for this funny moment at the zoo...

Mommy: Syd, would you like to take a picture with the turkey?

Syd: Yes!

Mommy: Okay, move a little closer to the fence and say Cheeeese!

Syd: HEY TURKEY! SAY CHEESE!

ZOO

19

Dear Syd,

Thank you for this bedtime moment...

Syd comes into Zach's room.

Me: Get in your bed, Syd. It's time to go to sleep!

Syd: (Lays on floor with his blanket) Mommy?!

Me: Yes, Syd?

Syd: I sleepin'!

And for this early morning moment too...

Mooooooommyyyyyy, I weeeeaaaady! I wan go, go, go!

And Dear Syd,...

Thanks for being the best two year old YOU!

12404590R00013

Made in the USA
Charleston, SC
05 May 2012